Sacred Strategies: Bridging Spirituality and Management

Shubhi Sen

SHUBHI SEN

Copyright © 2024 Shubhi Sen.

Book Cover by Nadia Designer

Edited by Dr. Shibani Basu Dubey

SHUBHI SEN

Preface

Take a step forward of courage and God shall provide you with thousand-fold assistance. This book has been a result of my leap of faith. This book is a culmination of managing our daily lives personally or being a part of an organisation with spirituality. From the insights of my 20 years of life, it weaves together the lessons to navigate the management skills in our lives with spiritual principles.

Brahma Kumaris serves as an epitome of managing its operations with harmony across the world. This Spiritual University took birth after Dada Lekhraj, a retired Indian Businessman who is now lovingly referred to as Brahma Baba, had a series of visions of the radiating light of God. In 1936, he opened a school named "Om Mandali" where virtuous and meditative practices were taught. Entrusting his property and financial resources to a group of eight women, he put the young ladies to forefront to handle the administrative roles while spreading the knowledge of world renewal through self-transformation and Rajyoga meditation. The group moved to its current headquarters in Mount Abu in 1950 where a unique curriculum about Soul, God and Time was developed.

Progressing further, after Brahma Baba left his mortal coil in 1969, Dadi Prakashmani Ji along with Didi Manmohini, handled the administrative responsibilities to open centres across the nation for spiritual upliftment. While Dadi Janki Ji was sent for service abroad where along with BK Jayanti, she overcame the linguistic barriers to become a beacon of love, peace and wisdom.

The Brahma Kumaris is an international non-governmental organisation of the United Nations having six affiliations with them to promote global peace. Extending its presence to 120+ nations, it is the largest women-led spiritual organisation that helps people irrespective of their caste, colour, gender, religion or nationality to discover its latent relationship with the virtues of goodness. It fosters a deeper understanding of the soul's power to lead a peaceful and prosperous life, while maintaining a state of inner calm and harmony with the external environment.

Through its centres across the globe, Brahma Kumaris offers a 7-day course in Rajyoga meditation along with various lectures, seminars and workshops to bring together the individuals from varied professions and age groups. It does its part in protecting the environment through the adoption of various sustainable practices.

Known prominently for wearing white, practising open-eyed meditation and greeting with "Om Shanti", the Brahma Kumars and Kumaris reflect the inner aspirations towards leading a life of honesty, purity and simplicity.

The number to connect to God is 000. The zero that represents the infinite light of the Supreme Soul while the other is the symbol of our radiating soul. The third zero requires us to put a full stop to our past so that our mind may not be fogged with futile thoughts. As you begin realising the power of these zeroes, your connection with the God increases.

This book outlines my approach to management, illustrates how Brahma Kumaris has exemplified its principles, and a question at the end of each chapter to let you decide your next course of action.

SHUBHI SEN

Table of Contents

10

Tomorrow is a myth!

Time Management

Time is not money and tomorrow is just a noun. While most people equate time with money, I certainly do not agree to that. You can earn your money, buy Porsche, glide in your private swimming pool and fly to Hawaii but you can certainly not swallow a pill of time that will give you that 1 hour of extra time in the 24-hour cycle or buy it off on the streets of Times Square.

While a person works hard to make his money, the result of his hard work is relative to how effectively he managed his time. Time cannot be earned, it's a given equal entity. A bankrupt businessman can employ strategic ways to gain back his lost income but a person who wasted time can never gain it back. If viewed from the eyes of a poor then time may have equal value like money but still the two entities do not seem correlated as the majority of the poor remain poor due to their reckless management of time and the rich seem to buy off everything due to their abundance of money. Time is how well you make of it.

You see, "will" is a four-lettered word but the way it is employed in your language can have a huge impact on how you actually interpret it.

Your will takes you to the aim,
"I will" takes you farther away from it.

Your commitment and unquenchable thirst to achieve your aim lets you see only the target and anything else that takes you away from it as a distraction. When the fuel of your desire lower downs, the evil of procrastination hits in and your statement changes to "I will", "I will do this tomorrow", "It's just a small task, I will manage to do it tomorrow" and the list of "I wills" to push it and relax down on Netflix makes a difference for you in the whole world.

Tomorrow is a myth, it never comes. In the Hindi language the word for yesterday and tomorrow is the same, कल. As there's always a probability for a tomorrow, the tomorrow passes as soon as you think it will become yesterday. The cycle of time starts with "will", because although it may sound a cliché, while you lag off, someone else is still working to pass over you and achieve what he/she wants. It's a harsh reality but you have never wanted it so badly in the first place that is making you regret it after the time has passed. Everybody yearns for an O grade, applaud on the stage, a gold medal in the record, a perfect beautiful body and skin, code without a bug and a position of CEO with a straight track, what one is not ready to accept is the compromise on comfort it brings and the rugged road where your tyre will get punctured even endless times to reach the destination. It's about who is willing to endure it all, sacrifice more than required and have patience to finally taste success?

Breaking down what the hands of time desire

T   –   Tough
I   –   Intelligent
M   –   Management
E   –   Earnest

Tough

Life throws pebbles at you, even harshly it may stab you with knives, rip you apart only just to keep your mere existence loosely together. It tests you every second, to see whether you can make it or give it all away for your pain that will last only for a few days. Toughness is an ability that is developed, a strength that gets sharpened with the more you endure. To gain strength from the weakness, not get victimised and blemished into destroying and achieving things the wrong way.

Being a single daughter to my parents, I've been raised as much as a princess as a warrior. My Dad always tells me that as flowery as youth looks like, while you wait to relish on its fragrance and beauty, the garden of your future years is getting withered. A person who has not cried of the tears of toughness he endured can never truly experience what the elixir of your sacrifices churned it into. Give yourself a day when it gets rough, collect your thoughts, prioritise things and keep the clock in check. Becoming tough will give you an emotional strength no one other than time can teach you, you just have to remember to stand up again because at the end of the day it is only you who owes your life and can make it.

The trait of being tough has been demonstrated by the *Brahma Kumaris* since the beginning. It is a women led spiritual organisation where Brahma Baba formed a Managing Committee of eight women and surrendered all his property and assets to a Trust administered by them. While the initial Om Mandali gathered many women who came to attend classes, this raged their fathers, husbands and brothers. A women led organisation was against the eyes of all. Females were beaten at home and the place where Om Mandali was held caught fire one day. The faith in the Supreme Soul and in the greater vision of peace gave them strength to endure it all and become tough; to keep moving ahead despite the obstacles.

Intelligent

Making a wise choice or choosing to ignore it all rests all upon you. Your body is worked by your soul. Albeit, in some situations it may seem like the conditions governed your decisions but that is just an excuse one makes for oneself. Remember, there's always a way and always an excuse to either work through it or go back to coil up yourself on the couch, the decision is yours to make. Intelligence is not something which is measured by your IQ but your abilities to acquire and apply necessary skills.

Nanaji (maternal grandfather) being a devout member of the Brahma Kumaris was a passionate hockey player, his hockey stick was the supporter of his life and the ball that guided its path. Time casts its reality and none can escape the realities it reveals. Due to low economic budget and the added responsibility of a family after marriage, he thought his time wasn't valid to be spent on sport where his family won't be able to live a standard life. His decision at the right time to shift to a stable occupation not only fortunately turned out to be successful as a career for him but taught the invaluable lesson of how time can change the fate of the game called life.

Writing letters to Baba and Dadis has always been a loved tradition in Brahma Kumaris where people share their ideas, queries, and thoughts. Dadi Janki Ji used to receive a lot of letters from the souls in India and abroad to which she lovingly replied. Though, a few people dangled their faith in the Supreme Father and questioned the institution's workings and fundings. A few journalists and reporters also raised their suspicions on these matters. Responding to them with intelligent replies while remaining indifferent to such negative doubts, she maintained her stable belief and trust on the Almighty who has been helping all along in the functioning of it all. Her time was more invested in blessing the souls and doing *Sewa*. This unshakeable trust in the doctrines of the Supreme Soul has helped utilise the institution's time in spreading the knowledge of God and radiating peace.

Management

Time itself entails in itself the entity of management. Let me explain this with an example, do you have a messy closet, with all varieties of clothes entangled to form a clutter? Well, if your answer is a no then you are already half-way through but if your answer is a yes, let's understand the concept behind that now. You always seem to run out of space for new clothes when you look at the unkempt heaves of apparels. Begin with making tidy folds of them, arrange them in an ordered way and voila! You have got space now. Likewise, is the management of time, it seems messy when it is not properly arranged but once you have prioritised and put things in order, you find yourself revealing extra time just like extra space.

The art of prioritisation relies on your ability to differentiate between tasks. Your goals are attained when they are hit by the arrows of your tasks. Imagine the three types of tasks: urgent, important and regular. The arrow head has urgent tasks needed to be done first, followed by important tasks that make up the shaft and lastly, the regular tasks making the nock or the end of the arrow.

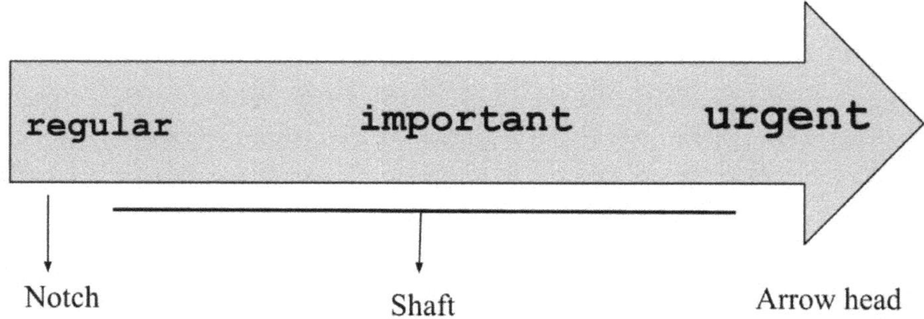

Let's understand this through a scenario, in October 2023 during the annual spiritual meet at the headquarters of Brahma Kumaris in Mt. Abu approximately 5,000 people arrived from the Indore Zone. There arose an issue of lack of water supply. Every individual also receives a *Saugat* (gift) every year which encountered a shortage in supply from the warehouse in that duration. To tackle this situation, the management prioritised tasks which involved solving the water supply issue on first basis with additional water tankers as water is the basic necessity in every work. Followed by this was the significant issue of gift supplies which were catered to in a day. As evident, water requirement was deemed as urgent, followed by the issue of gifts as an important task which needed attention but could wait till the urgent task was accomplished. The regular tasks which are although small still need to be done on a daily basis to ensure that your routine is on road.

Earnest

Does being serious collide with your life's way that seems without spice and flavour? Being earnest is more than being intense, it is about being disciplined. Now what does discipline actually mean? If we need to really fit our goals with the fun of life, it's about achieving your daily targets rather than sticking to the stern hands of time to achieve it only in a specific hour of the day. For instance, I need to ideally complete two essays for my assignment in 1 hour so that the time schedule matches for the upcoming finals. I have already started with my first essay when I get a reminder that the laundry closes in an hour. The ability to curb your mind to focus on the task you're doing is the skill. Because, if your mind does wander, it will be sailing on two boats. The key to managing this is that I finish my first essay in 20 minutes, go and do laundry, and when I return, I complete my second essay within the remaining time of 40 minutes. It's about finding a way out rather than whimpering over the problems that have come together. It takes two to tango so you need a balance if you want your life to dance in beautiful movements.

Well, how do Brahma Kumaris stay earnest? Soul is the charioteer of the reins of mind. It has got the capacity to control every instinct if one builds it for. Starting off with *Amrit Vela* (meditation at dawn) at 3:30 a.m. the Brahma Kumars and Kumaris attend the *Murli* class which imbibes them with the nectar of wisdom. Following this daily schedule of spirituality and Raja Yoga Meditation, the souls also have spare time in between to fulfil their worldly duties and do *seva*. They ensure that their corporeal responsibilities towards the world are met along with their incorporeal revival. For instance, a Brahma Kumar who is a government servant does not compromise his tasks at the workplace, and strikes a balance in his schedule while remaining earnest to both aspects of his life.

Endless loop of over justification, make it or break it?

Procrastination is evil, some people don't realise it even exists until it has already demolished the shell of their time they've been saving up. We as humans have an innate tendency or bias to justify our actions to maintain the state of contentment that whatever we are doing is right.

When we delay tasks, we think that it is ok to spend a few minutes more on leisure, that we have got some more time left. But are these justifications true or just some self-satisfying dubious statements?

People tend to leave just enough time so that they are able to achieve the ordinary and then watch videos, read tips and listen to podcasts on how to be extraordinary. When talking about preparing for an exam, a student has got 4 days of study leave to prepare for it. He spends the first day on entertainment thinking that after a difficult previous exam, he deserves it. The second day seems to get drained just like that with only a little amount of productivity. The third day, his time is spent on trying to focus while justifying that he has still got an entire day left. He is overburdened on the last day but somehow manages to study enough to reminisce about the key points. He scores a B and brushes off the fact that it could have been better had he used his time efficiently. This is how you enter in the vicious loop of over justifications which has claws of sweet leisure clinging onto you.

We often forget to realise the power of the small shining light that centres our forehead, the soul. With soul-conscious living, we can gain the ability to recognise our strengths and weaknesses and to work upon them. When you start living mindfully through your soul, it becomes easy to understand the wrong and the right as those with body consciousness tend to find ways to comfort their bodies. A soul realises the proper balance between work and recreation. It takes efforts, sacrifices to break through this cycle which can even feel like bleeding injuries on the initial days but once you are persistent, you will not feel the pain but pleasure that stands at the end of truly being extraordinary.

Zeitopia - **A land where your life ticks**

Fern was born in a world where time ruled the destiny of people. It was not the green bills that made the humans wealthy but time that actually decided who *can* be rich. A clock on the forearms of the beings that ticked with every second that passed. It's a wonder how every second becomes past just in a blink. Fern was one of the many individuals who was born with a clock on her arm that reflected 53:8:16:28, 53 years 8 months 16 weeks and 28 days tick, tick, tick.

Time and money went hand in hand except that procrastination will never be an option if you want to survive, life on beds of roses and not the thorns that hide beneath it.

Similar was the case of Scarlett, he was born with a timeline of just 28 years. Growing up he had to burn a candle at both ends if he wanted to leave a mark on the society. Going through rugged phases of life, Scarlett had to earn money so that his upcoming generations could be supported. Devoid of any leisure, his life lingered between the numbers that ran backwards. Birthdays for people like him after the age of 10, felt as the twisted turns of a cyclone from where the plunge in the ultimate darkness won't be far. A straight line of the heartbeat was feared less than the haunting symmetry of the numbers that would ultimately open the gates to its hollow end.

While Fern had all the income as time in her fortune, she could be all she wanted to be; education, high-school prom, cheering out at concerts, grabbing the dream job and a satisfied life. As opposed to this, Scarlett was obliged to skip the good parts and become what the time constraints required him to be.

Analogous is the case of life, just as the name of Fern symbolises resilience and vitality, so can the times of our lives be best made out. It's your take to bounce back on life with vital spirits rather than getting tangled up in the web of problems. Scarlett represents sacrifice and courage. Acceptance is a trait that is built and inculcated. Accepting that you've committed a lag on your schedule with the utter determination to still achieve your aim will make your sacrifices worthy. Time lost can definitely not be gained back but with courage to move ahead and sacrifices as your penalty, its value can be earned back.

Imagine time as a flower bed of daisies, it has layers. Starting with pleasant colours that soothe your mind, comes next the humus or soft soil supporting the flower plants. Moving downwards on the layers we have topsoil holding the roots of the plants and then with gradual decrement there is an increase in the number of coarse materials ultimately leading to the bedrock. The hours seem to be ample enough to complete your tasks just like the daisies. A few minutes lost does not count in the overall budget of time. With a few hours lost, you still hold onto the remaining clock just as the topsoil holds the roots. But when it starts draining, you find yourself ending up in the coarse level being hit by the stones of anxiety, pressure and stress ultimately hitting rock bottom.

This indefinite cycle of time progresses where you are the gardener who decides to either uphold the gratifying sight or let the cracks of barrenness appear. Proper prioritisation and scheduling of tasks will help you maintain life in beautiful shades.

Tomorrow is a myth. How do you prove it wrong then?

Once you get entangled in the process of *doing it tomorrow,* the only way to come out of that tornado is when you decide to step out. Stepping out will require courage, force and most importantly your will. The chains that kept you shackled in the sugary spot of comfort will break; they will feel deliberately wounding yourself. But wounds gained in the process of success become scars and scars are like the souvenirs of a fighter.

Set dates

Instead of saying that it shall be done tomorrow, start setting dates. When you assign dates to tasks, they act like deadlines and those are believed to give pressure. A man best works under pressure. When you will see that you are approaching the end date, your mind will make you realise that a task needs to get done.

Take help but don't become a parasite

When you seem loaded with tasks, take help. Working independently is absolute but asking for help when in dire need is completely fine too. When there is an essential job and your mind just can't seem to focus, use the focus mode, the forest app which will restrict you from getting distracted in the apps that act as obstacles. But watch out, don't become a parasite that only when the focus mode is enabled is my mind able to concentrate, last moment tasks can't be done without ChatGPT, NO. That's where your courage comes into play, gradually building up the habit while taking aid of these technologies initially.

Let's understand through a case, Stacy's brother always helped her out during her last moment projects. She remained so relaxed that whatever may be the scenario her brother will always be there to help her out until one day he moved to another country for work. Being unable to contact him due to the time difference, Stacy found herself stranded in the desert. Her performance deteriorated and backlogs piled up. One moment when she finally realised that she wants her personal identity to be established was she able to amend the habit.

Set timers

When we see that we have time, our pace of finishing a task slows down. Start setting timers for your work. In the start, you may find it difficult and not even get the work completed in that stipulated time but what's achieved without practice? Setting timers will gradually allow you to maximise productivity in a time period that will save more of your time.

Game of the mind. Aim or Lame?

The senses through which you experience the world around you, which opens the windows of pleasure and life also have the contradicting ability to jail you behind those bars of glee. Desires that lure the mind plunge you into the pool of temptations. We as Brahma Kumaris are told to spin the discus of self-realisation. When you have the discus in your hands, a soul conscious mind, you will have the power to control your mind.

As per Hindu mythology, Lord Vishnu always had this discus rotating on his forefinger. When a wicked or evil spirit committed sins that affected the balance of earth, God Vishnu would throw his discus that would lead to its destruction. From this we can infer that when the discus of your mind is in your hand, you rule the game, you strive towards your aim but when the moment it is released from your hand, this discus has the ability to make you lame.

Mastering the mind and realisation of your true potential and desires will never allow you to be engulfed in temptations.

Value of Time

If you want to realise the value of time, then ask from the following people:

1 year – A patient with stage 4 cancer who has only got a year left of his life.

1 month – The mother whose baby got a heart disease just because it was born one month prior.

1 week – A father who waits an entire week to visit his family and home at the weekend.

1 hour – The long-distance couple who are waiting to meet at the airport.

1 minute – A person who couldn't catch a flight and missed an important meeting.

1 second – A person who just avoided an accident.

1 millisecond – A sportsperson who won a silver medal in the Olympics.

Choose your hard

A balanced life would entail the efficient management of time, leaving ample space for you to indulge in leisure whereas procrastination burdens you with all the bricks of tasks at once making you say that 24 hours are not enough!

A few years of sacrifice with a lavish life afterwards?
Extravagant years with struggles waiting ahead?
Choose your hard.

Lead the way with Flowers

Leadership

Nature has the widest colour palette and the most alluring shades are found in flowers. While some of the flora grows in a conditioned environment, others just spring up out of rocky hills and between cracked surfaces. Those flowers are the evidence that beauty can emerge from toughness. Not everybody has the soft soil of amenities laid out for them, conditioned with fertilisers. Just like these species of flowers, a few leaders are born out of adverse conditions.

Life pricks you with needles, some of the experiences shatter you to your bones, a few of them get etched on your memory while others leave scars. Do you know what is common among them all? Experience.

The stitches of recovery represent the inherent powers that were a part of your soul all along. They are proof that strength lies dormant inside of you.

Cactus flowers are a rare sight. Those flowers with intricate design exhibiting beauty depict the existence of life and endurance in the scorching heat of the desert. Great leaders are like them. Their methods are as cruel as the sun and desolate as a desert but the austerity of cactus holds the capability of resilience to withstand all the severe conditions. From time immemorial, humanity has witnessed the shades of success and glee after sacrifices and hardships. Cactus flowers are the tangible evidence of nature. A team under such a leader knows how to mindfully tackle it all.

During a road trip, I was fascinated by the multicoloured flowers that emerged between mossy rocks beside a restaurant. The then 7-year-old me tempted by the clusters of tiny flowers forming a floret was stopped from plucking it by my grandmother. Apparently, Lantana is a species of wildflower which could cause reactions if touched and inhaled. Just like this vibrant flower, some leaders employ tactics which may look flashy at first, but are detrimental to the interests of others.

This juxtaposition is to help state the fact that there exists a dynamic variety of leaders. Under the various kinds of leadership, civilisations and societies have faced upgrades and downfalls. One such leader's name is often held synonymous to the brutal techniques he used that resulted in the dark era of humanity. Leadership is characterised by the ability to influence and inspire others.

Dandelion

People often tend to equate adjustment with compromise and discomfort. Does it mean giving up on your views and forgetting your desires for the sake of the other person? This style which incorporates in itself self-sacrifice is accommodating. The ability to accept the ideologies of others while politely stating yours for harmony is known as Adjustment.

The group of people a leader gets to lead voluntarily or involuntarily may not always be to his liking. Each individual brings a different set of opinions to the table and even challenges the norms. Moreover, leaders are faced with a dilemma on making the decisions that will gain profit. A decision should not always be based on short-term benefits but rather for long-term gains even if the process is gradual. Adjusting to such matters requires acceptance, not with a discontent heart but as a being who places belief in the situations. Good leaders value teammates who raise challenging questions. They do not see it as their violation of authority but rather a shift towards change.

After the demise of Dadi Prakashmani Ji, Dadi Janki Ji was appointed as the Chief Administrative Head of the Brahma Kumaris. Migrating from London to India after 40 years of long stay abroad would sound like a drastic change to anyone. BK Hansa, the helper of Dadi Janki too found the change to be hard but Dadi soulfully followed her principle of *"Haan ji"* which means saying yes to every situation happily without a sense of discomfort. Where did she get this power of adjustment from? It was her firm belief in God, who made her walk as a medium of service on every path laid by him.

Prominent leaders emerge while making their way out of unfavourable conditions. They adjust to the opposing conditions. Dandelions are known for this quality of survival and adaptability. Their resilient nature develops their ability to survive in adversity. It is associated with wishes and the power of manifestation. Be a leader like a dandelion, the one who accepts and flows lightly in the different winds of life.

Hydrangeas

While on a trip to Dalhousie, the roadside was ablaze with myriad hues of hydrangeas. Their lush clusters of blossoms captivated my mind. Beside their aesthetic appeal, they symbolised the elegance of organisation. When a leader is one amongst the team members and not the one in a team, one will not just be teammates but collaborators and friends who converge in one direction.

Everybody has to deal with the tangled wires of earphones and charger. Is it easy to carry and detangle them when they are a mess? Certainly not, as a properly organised chord coiled in a loop is feasible to carry and saves the seconds of your valuable time.

BK Sisters fluent in English language were organised together to selflessly serve the souls across the globe by reminding them of their innate powers. They were further joined by more sisters who under the leadership of regional leaders aided in the augmentation of services to the foreign citizens. This power of organisation transcended the linguistic and geographical barriers.

Sunflower

Organisation's goals are always the motive behind individuals working towards achieving their tasks. However, be the cause, the aim which a group of people genuinely support. The ray of light they will turn towards, a light that will never lead them to the depths of darkness. As the sunflower turns towards the sun because of its blazing light and strength, so must a leader be a torch bearer of absolute truth and vigour.

During the construction of the Diamond Hall, Dadi Prakashmani Ji went to the site twice a day for 3 months to give *Drishti* (vibrations) and *toli* (God's sweet) to each one. Her personal care and attention as a leader were the reason behind the motivation of all that uplifted their weary spirits. They turned to her whenever they faced any hardships.

A good leader is not afraid of the mighty waves rather he is mindful in the maintenance of his crew.

Dadi Prakashmani Ji was the source of inspiration for BK Jayanti (CEO, Brahma Kumaris UK), BK Nirmala (Regional Coordinator, Asia-Austral region) and BK Mohini (Regional Coordinator, America) when they were struggling in their initial days to spread spiritual knowledge abroad. Her constant motivation and unwavering belief in God helped them become the instruments of service across the world.

Swim with cooperation
- Belongingness towards the leader

Dolphins travel in groups called pods. Each pod has a leader. But why are we into dolphins now? Because leadership amongst dolphins is based on social bonding rather than stern dominance. Leaders in dolphin pods relay information about the possible predatory threats and navigating ways for hunting. Their ability to communicate effectively helps coordinate the activities of other members. A leader would be successful in his ventures when the people he directs can proudly say that we were led by a leader who demonstrated reverence by never underestimating us. Leadership is a two-way process. When a leader offers trust, he gains the belief. When the folks feel belonged, cooperation comes natural to them. It fosters unity and collective action.

During the former years of 1980s when Dadi Janki Ji resided in the UK to spread the power of Raja Yoga Meditation, the doctor conveyed that both her eyes need to be operated upon as her vision has reduced significantly. Apparently, the man who was also a doctor, when questioned by Dadi as to why did he pay £ 3000 for her surgery, replied with - "Because you are my mother".

Train of Endeavours

Trains hold the inspiring concept of togetherness, different organised compartments moving on wheels, joined together to forge ahead. People place their trust on the leader. None of them rides the train but all of them have faith in the ride. A long train has different coaches, one for storage, one as a pantry, while others carry the passengers. This symbolises the different skill sets a leader may require to keep moving ahead to reach the station. The storage compartment symbolises the resources one might need. Medium of strength is the pantry to enable us to equip with necessary energy.

The engine is the leader. He is the catalyst of connectivity who pulls the coaches towards the destination. Just like an engine is vital for the train, so is the leader for their people. Without an engine, the locomotive remains static not realising its potential to be mobile. Similarly, the inherent talents of people get exposed when identified and polished by a leader.

Trains keep moving forward. On its journey, a barren desert landscape outside does not stay permanent. It passes through scenes of dense forests, arid areas, dingy caves and glimmering villages showing that change is constant. Light will follow darkness when the train passes out of that phase. Trains move only forwards establishing the prominently said statement that little progress is still progress. Even slow trains travel their paths to reach their goals. Success may come gradual but a consistent movement ensures that it is near.

After Brahma Baba left his mortal body, he entrusted Dadi Prakashmani Ji to transform humanity by invoking the inner values of the beings. It was due to her that Brahma Kumaris gained prominence as the largest Spiritual Organisation efficiently run and managed by women. Her enigmatic personality led the organisation to spread the knowledge about the Supreme Soul to more than 100 countries. The tracks were the paths laid out by God and Dadi Prakashmani travelled on his will as a trustee.

Make your own garden, lead yourself

Leadership is not an entity valid to be only applied to a group of individuals. One can lead the mind which is perceived to be the master of the human body. We view the world around us with the help of our senses. We acquire skills as we move ahead in life. Growing up, we often find ourselves standing at a crossroad. That is the moment when one needs to lead his soul towards making the right decision which usually involves the entry into the discomfort house. No internet browser can open the number of tabs as fast as the human brain. Consequently, we get lost in the maze of thoughts forgetting to focus on the pathways that will lead us out.

Who says self-leadership does not involve leading teams? Well, certainly they are not a team of humans but your skills. Circumstances are your teachers and making decisions your exam. The goal is to make a *thoughtful* decision. You need to gather up your relevant skills and control the senses that pull you back to your soft-cosy couch of comfort. It may sound like a hassle initially, but the results at the end turn out to be beautiful.

Let me make this clearer by a situation that I faced during my 12th grade. Being a teenager, there was constant strife of emotions in my mind. The past scarring experiences chose a very inappropriate time for their revival. My surgery aggravated the circumstances for a student studying science. Spirituality guided me out into realising that I am bigger than the problems. If they have piled up as a mountain, then I behold the skills to cross it. During those days, the American web series "The Good Doctor" had me watching it regularly. It was an escape I found away from reality. The doctors devising ways to save their patients' lives provided with the pseudo relief of goodness for a few hours.

However, my academics demanded more concentration from me. It was the hour I realised that I needed to lead myself to success this time. Meditation succoured the anxiety and calmed my racing thoughts. I gradually brought alive my adjustment skills to cope with the wavering schedule between hospital and classes. The power of endurance emerged as I contemplated over the circumstances. The toughest one was to divert my mind to restrain from indulging in things acting as escapism. While the web series would remain stagnant with all its episodes on the net, my life would certainly move onto new dimensions.

This team of attentiveness, adjustment, endurance and self-discipline helped me excel in my exams. I led a team of skills that were hidden behind the clouds of doubt and distractions.

Did you notice the word "thoughtful" italicised above before decision? Making your garden won't come without barriers. Failure is like an unwanted pimple that pops up to ruin your clear skin. It is inevitable in human life. A well manured soil can still be attacked by pests. You cannot predict the probability and time of its arrival. There will be weeds and extreme weather conditions that may lodge down your plants but this is not the end. You toil it with care and detail to develop a solution. Rule out the distractions, water your positivity and fertilise your skills to regain what has been lost. Do it with the right intentions, give it your all. The doors to your enchanting garden will open as you keep on unlocking the possible chains of difficulties.

Sow the seeds, lay the path with care
Day by day, watch it bloom into flowers
Turn a blind eye and witness
Desiccated branches let death take its share.

What ingredients make a great leader?

Have **L**ove, show kindness and embrace the imperfectly perfect parts.
Rouse up the spirits, be **E**nergetic. Diffuse your ambitions.
Karma is echoed. An **A**ltruistic attitude keeps you grounded.
Mould in diverse situations. Being **D**ecisive is the real test.
Be **E**ncouraging, the vital salt of any dish.
Real eyes **R**ealise. Reflect on the crashes and progress.

Dadi Prakashmani Ji was honoured with the Peace Messenger Award by the Secretary General of the UN in 1987 due to her outstanding abilities as a woman leader appealing for world peace through spiritual service. The Million Minutes of Peace Appeal was the most significant international project that led to the widespread acknowledgement of a Spiritual University making people realise their true virtues. The project aimed at bringing together people from different rungs of the social ladder to participate in a thoughtful movement. Souls across the globe were asked to pledge minutes of their time in positive thinking, prayers and meditation. The accumulated wealth of optimistic thoughts was added in the 'World Peace Bank' which exceeded its set expectations to reach 2,344 years of peace! This was presented to the then United Nations Secretary General Javier Perez de Cuellar in 1986.

Dadi Ji's slogan of leading through *mind, mouth* and *move* created global impact ascertaining the United Nations that their goal of World Peace aligns with the aspirations of the Brahma Kumaris. The power of thoughts has the ability to inspire and influence. The power of speech to speak sweetly and convey the message in a few honest words will foster cooperation. The soul-conscious steps as an instrument of God will never let your wings of motivation get destroyed.

Leaders cascade their fruits of skills to make better leaders, a leader who will fail but work on its garden again to turn it into the beauty it was destined for.

Choose your hard

Leadership involves making adjustments, managing your work with the leader's directions which may not always suit you. It may vary from your ideologies and so may your comforts. A body-conscious mind desires ease which is temporary and one may feel unsettled when exposed to the realities of life which is a rugged road.

A rose with thorns?
A lotus without water?
Choose your hard.

Divided We Unite

Teamwork

7 continents, 4 oceans, 195 nations, 8 billion people and 1 world. What is that keeps us together? Is it the mutual goal to maintain world peace? It is the recognition that man is gregarious and humanity flourishes in companionship.

From the forge of celestial fire, amidst the cosmic silence, the hand of creation sculpted the earth, carved streams, exhaled the ethereal air and matter coalesced, birthing a world where life would blossom. The 5 elements of nature: earth, water, fire, air and space joined forces to weave together the tapestry of the world. Since time immemorial, nature has been an example of how the varied elements maintain balance for the survival on this planet.

What defines teamwork? Is it just working towards a common goal? The balance of traits, ladder of skills, north star of hope and essence of being valued knits the fabric of teamwork. Trust forms the bedrock upon which teamwork thrives. At first, a person may feel insecure while opening up and sharing his ideas. But a mutual understanding to walk towards the same road of success will foster cooperation. The boat of trust may shake and wobble, but it never sinks.

We all have a touch of biology tucked away from our middle school, don't we? The different organs and their systems in our body help us correlate how a team with individuals of varied skill sets align their objectives together to function the human body. Our skin envelops our entire body, acting as the first layer of shield, much like a team leader protects their team members from external threats and steers them to their potential. The digestive system acts as a member to churn out the resources to extract outputs vital for accomplishing the results. Just as the circulatory system distributes oxygen, hormones and nutrients to all parts of the body, teamwork facilitates the movement of skills and resources that everyone needs to work effectively. Each member of a team makes the framework like the skeletal system, supporting and balancing workloads when one falls out. The nervous system transmits signals similar to teamwork that relies on effective communication channels to coordinate and reach the destination.

With the inauguration of Diamond Hall at Shantivan Mt. Abu set on 31st December, 1996, the construction initially demanded ten months more. However, with only one-third of the structure being completed in five months due to the lack of pillars and semi-circular roof, Dadi Prakashmani Ji devised the Chief Engineer to form teams catering to stage construction, flooring, roofing, light and sound. She advised the brothers to provide her with the required number of labours and material so that they could work in three 8-hour shifts each day to accomplish their goal on the given deadline.

Segregation of people based on their skills into different groups enabled the construction of this magnificent hall in just 8 months making the impossible possible. Cooperative efforts and determination coupled with time management and belief in God have the ability to accomplish any task.

Runway to success

The system of aviation serves as a rational model to understand the different kinds of teamwork. From ground control to flight crew, thousands of individuals are employed to ensure that the flights reach their locations safely. Communication is the engine of a plane. A team cannot soar high to success when the engine of its communication starts to sputter. Essential meetings for the exchange of ideas and reports on progress act as a fuel to this process.

Altitude and attitude are the wings of any aircraft. Right attitude towards the team members and the set objectives ensures to reach the set altitude; either one of the wings falters and the team's descent begins. As a group moves forward, it may encounter the jolts and jarring movements of challenges and intra-group conflict. Everything seems to be in a chaotic blur when the journey ahead seems rough. But, remember, everything has a phase. Just keep moving, keep trying, sit together with your team and the ways will be navigated out. Turbulence will lead to triumph.

The flight takes off against the wind, not with it. Courage lies in facing the storm, not exiting it.

"In the event of a sudden loss of cabin pressure, oxygen masks will drop down from the overhead compartment. Please secure your own mask first before assisting others." When working in a team, ensure that you are equipped with the necessary resources and enough time to complete your given set of tasks. Once you have finished your work ahead of the deadline or have buffer time, assist other team mates with their challenges. You cannot walk two roads simultaneously. Not only will this lead to losing your path but ruin the road further. Offering help and providing suggestions

fosters cooperation, but abandoning your work completely may lead to negative outcomes. Exceptional cases do arrive if you have mastered the art of time management to tackle it all.

Control tower plays a crucial role in providing clearance signals for take-off and landing, and uses radar systems to track position and prevent collisions. Just as the control room is essential, don't hesitate to ask for help from your colleagues or even from specialised external resources to aid you in the process.

Passengers from diverse backgrounds board the same flight. They carry luggage of varied masses and types: the weight of their parents' expectations, the bags of their aspirations, sleek trolley cases to stand out and backpacks that hold the allure of a lifestyle they have yet to experience. Each individual comes with different ambitions and unique skills, uniting together as a team to land at the same destination bringing them one step closer to their achievements.

CART - Creating Cohesive Teams

A team crosses the finish line when their cart is driven by four wheels: **C**ommunication, **A**ccountability, **R**esolution of conflicts and **T**rust.

1. Communication

Ineffective communication between team members can create potholes on the road where your cart may get stuck. Here's an example to showcase you that:

Ron: Tell Linda that she needs to make changes in the project goal to include all the quantitative indicators of success.
Tess: Sure, Ron! I will do that.

Tess: Hey Linda! Since you were absent in the last team meeting, Ron has asked you to make some changes to the Project Charter you submitted yesterday.
Linda: Okay. I will do that and report back to him. Thank you.

Firstly, it can be perceived that Tess lacked the key aspect of effective communication, that is, active listening. Additionally, she did not clarify the instruction in order to avoid coming across as inattentive, which led her to conveying ambiguous message to Linda. Furthermore, Linda did not engage in acquiring the concise changes that were needed to be made.

Improper relaying of information can have a snowball effect, which is the increment in the size of the problems, much like a snowball accumulating more snow as it rolls downhill.

Active listening entails lending not just your ears but your mind to analysing the story instead of forming opinions. Barriers to this process may arise due to racing thoughts and distractions but be brave enough to apologise and ask again. Empathetic listening is based on absorbing the perspectives of others rather than just waiting for your turn to speak. An efficient team will thrive when all its members are heard. This will ensure their contribution as a part of the group. When a team engages in effective communication, people are likely to hear things that may challenge their views or previously held beliefs and suggest a change in norms. Have an open mind to accept all the realms of possibilities.

Trust, Listen and Don't Control.

A good team's communication is based on politeness. Ensure that your tone is pleasant and your body language attentive. Individuals often come across as rude either due to their personal issues or a dislike for a particular member. One significant thing that spirituality has taught me is that souls come with their inherent traits, choosing to change them or control the situations will affect my state of mind. The choice to keep the line distinct between your work and personal emotions lies in your command.

Speak less, speak slowly and speak sweetly.

Select your words wisely to transmit your message in high energy so that they are valued. Avoid speaking in a hurry to cause confusion, be clear in your transmission and structure. A raised voice creates tension which affects the productivity of others whereas a sweet voice with strong words will not only impress people but attract cooperation.

Beware of personal filters and prejudices to not let them fog your decisions. Each team member is different, taking the non-verbal cues to interact with anyone in distress. Change into friendship mode, when their fuel seems to be running out.

2. Accountability

Responsibility is given while Accountability is taken. Taking ownership of your mistakes requires much more strength than claiming your rewards. Accountability in a team is ensured in a team by establishing guidelines and procedures. Share of responsibilities and delivery of logical explanations for each of the team's actions checks for errors in between the process.

Accountability will feel like a dagger twisting inside your gut when you feel uncomfortable in acknowledging your errors. It takes courage to commit and humility to apologise.

Succeeding at once is excellent but do you know what's extraordinary? Amending your mistakes and rising from your failures by breaking the shackles of your limitations. Blaming a person will not lead you anywhere, brainstorming of solutions to overcome the obstacles will. Teamwork is like climbing a mountain with ropes connected to each other. When one person slips, the rest of the team pulls together to get him back on track.

When you own the trophy, you also own the wounds that brought you till the winning stand. Can a person take his trophy everywhere? No. Instead of hiding, you flaunt the scars from your journey to success, forever etched on your mind as symbols of victory. Teachings from failures are deeply engraved in our minds, often much more so than the preparations for success.

Accountability germinates from the seeds of commitment. Commitment finds no excuses but an honest promise to the fulfilment of goals. Positive commitment comes from the righteous approach to accept and amend, while negative commitment results in employing unethical ways to ensure success. One strength and one support by the Almighty provides a soul with hundred-fold power to cross the mountain of challenges. You just need to take a step forward with belief. Commitment to your old behaviour patterns and beliefs chain you from changing your value system. Change the formula to apply them to new levels of your life.

3. Resolving Conflicts

Disagreements when working in a team are inevitable. Our systems acquire satisfaction when our viewpoints are established and accepted by others as correct. Opposition feels like an underestimation to our potential and biases take control of our senses when determining success criteria. Don't let conflicts become the glue you stick onto, view conflicts as weeds that can be pulled out.

Conflict majorly arises due to contradictory ideas. Acceptance of effective ideas should not be hidden behind the clouds of pre-existing notions as different members have dynamic thought processes to approach a problem.

6 x 2 = 12

3 x 4 = 12

The method you do things and generate solutions is not the only way. Respect other people's thinking.

A tit for tat will drown both the ships. Mould yourself in different situations. Even though we have distinct nature, it is only when you are considerate for everything, your thoughts are victorious and your words are full of sweetness that you have an easy nature. Be humble to realise the true potentials of your soul to avoid concerning yourself with asking, "Why should I always be the first to initiate the action?" Approach conflicts with a calm and composed demeanour. Maintain transparency to avoid misunderstandings and demonstrate consideration for others' perspectives. Flexibility is the key to maintaining a cohesive team which at times involves adjustment and compromises to find a resolution acceptable to all.

Dig to the root cause of the problem and seek the help of a mediator when required. Solution will emerge only when the problem has been clearly defined.

Conflict resolution techniques build the culture of the workplace. Members feel valued rather than inferior, when their voices are heard.

Culture at the workplace is the anxiety level of employees on Sunday evenings about Monday mornings.

4. Trust

Trust fosters unity. It allows team mates to be vulnerable to each other to share a safe space. Flowers welcome bees because they rely on them for pollination while bees return for nectar, that's trust. Open dialogue and active listening inspire team members to unite, fostering a sense of support and reassurance that they can rely on each other during adversities. A team is not called a team because people work together, a sense of belonging towards the team is established when members trust and respect each other.

Trust promotes inclusivity where there is equity. It leads to the development of a collaborative environment where people feel confident to share their knowledge and skills without a threat of theft to their originalities. Without trust, individuals merely coordinate, it is trust that transforms a group of people into a team who collaborates efforts and skills to attain success.

Trust is a delicate two-way game. Make sure that the one you give an entry to your doors of trust doesn't enter with a knife. It can be even harder to develop when an individual comes from insecure relationships. But trust in a team does not ask you to open all your gates, just the ones that you know will help accelerate the team's growth. Mutual respect ensures that members feel safe to share their knowledge without hesitation and avoid entangling in the web of group consensus to suppress their ideas.

A team built on the bricks of trust is like a fortress,
unshakeable and resilient in the times of crisis.

A trustworthy environment facilitates delegation because trust comes with accountability. Empowered team members take ownership of their work which is a part of being honest. An honest and constructive feedback will enable team members to be vulnerable rather than taking the road of avoidance.

Leading by example was best demonstrated by Brahma Baba who surrendered all his property and assets to a Managing Committee of eight women who validated his trust by becoming beacons of peace, love and wisdom.

Delegation

When the work is divided on the basis of skills and capability with a trust to perform is known as delegation. Team leaders often divide tasks to multiply the results. While nothing is impossible, not everything is possible to be done alone. Alter the statement from "I'm possible" to "We make it Possible".

In the yesteryears, while in Europe, Dadi Janki Ji gave her lectures in Hindi and it was the coordinated efforts of other souls that made the transcendence beyond language possible outside the borders of India. BK Jayanti used to translate her words in English which were further translated to French, German and Spanish by other brothers and sisters. Delegation is the process of empowering everyone in the journey of life.

Delegation can be exemplified from the waterfall where resources like water flow from the top to reach the desired workers below. This ensures the availability of water; it is trust and accountability of an individual to make certain that it blooms into outcomes. Trust in the team members' abilities increases motivation and engagement. Appreciative statements and incentives help boost the morale of team members and augments mutual faith. A compliment with a smile runs as glucose in veins to surge the energy. On the flipside, incentives should be based on a timely fashion as excessive rewards lose their effect to seem as ordinary. Genuine recognition reinforces positive behaviours and encourages continuous improvement.

An open environment encompasses that team members feel safe and heard about their issues. They readily accept the suggestions and improvements without feeling undermined. This can be achieved when you don't interfere in other's style of working, not create doubt but be present with all the genuine support and guidance when they seek it. Every individual has varied but essential skill sets to roll the ball to the goal. With the power of belief, be open to new possibilities without sticking to your own way to be the only method to perform an activity correctly.

The unequal 5 fingers of your palm play the game, the dynamic team mates achieve the aim.

Streamlining workflow enables greater productivity commitment to tasks. While delegation aims to reduce burnout, there may be times when you may encounter the load of tasks higher than the others. It is at this moment where you need to place your potential above your ego. Some tasks are allotted to you because you possess the inherent skills to finish them with efficiency. Think beyond the limitations of physical capacity to connect to the Supreme Soul. The Doer (God) is getting everything done. We are just the instruments in his play. By connecting with him you will get armed with powers to finish your tasks.

Improper delegation needs to be dealt with by the leader to figure out other ways. Communicating your ideas and thoughts to other team members becomes crucial at this stage. When you feel overburdened, clearly state your issues and possible solutions. Requesting for buffer time or external help when in dire need will surely set your expectations straight. Anger and frustration at times like these will infect the harmony of the team. Politeness and pure intentions, though may seem to have a negligible effect on a person initially, are virtues which you can control.

Mistakes are a part of the process. When a team member gets stuck, emerge your virtue of patience and politeness to help the person guide through the way. Your vibrations of faith and success builds more capacity in people to achieve the task at hand.

Wings of Brahma Kumaris

The Rajyoga Education and Research Foundation is an educational and charitable society which aims to foster soul-consciousness, propagate Rajyoga education by organising various seminars and workshops ultimately uniting towards the common goal of world peace through self-transformation. It enables individuals from different fields of life to exchange ideas and brainstorm solutions for the problems plaguing the society.

1. Administrator's Service Wing
➢ It leads to spiritual empowerment of executives and administrators in the public and private institutions to help manage stress and free them from the apathy that encompasses their bureaucratic bondages. This enhances their quality of life and work through meditation.

2. Agriculture and Rural Development Wing
➢ This wing aims at the elimination of superstition and unhealthy practices through awareness lectures to inculcate the values of Rajyoga.
➢ Various medical camps and exhibitions are organised to reduce the number of addicts.
➢ It leads to the improvement of rural children and youth through value education along with the power of vibrations for qualitative farming

3. Art and Culture Wing
➢ It encourages artists to live a stress-free and drug-free lifestyle.
➢ Its major objective includes the involvement of human and spiritual values to stop moral degradation.

4. Business and Industry Wing
➢ It induces the consciousness of service and responsibility to humanity for global harmony.

➤ Working towards the betterment of humans over commercial gain is emphasised as an important aspect.
➤ It promotes ethical values in business.

5. Education Wing
➤ It focuses on empowering spiritually through educational training.
➤ To spread awareness with divinity

6. Information Technology Wing
➤ Voice the ideas of community through Radio
➤ Aid community service with communication technologies
➤ Introduce the concepts of meditation and spirituality in a gentle and practical way

7. Jurists Wing
➤ Foster lawfulness amongst citizens through spiritual education
➤ Developing a humane approach to criminals and maintaining ethics in justice

8. Media Wing
➤ To inspire media personnel to promote optimism
➤ Avoid the spread of biased and slandering news
➤ Promote the interest of the deprived sections of society

9. Medical Wing
➤ Research the impact of Rajyoga meditation on psycho-physical health
➤ Moral standard of conduct in medical professionals
➤ Raise awareness about meditation and holistic health

10. Politician's Service Wing

➢ Develop honesty and scrupulous means of work among politicians

➢ Adopt truthful ways of governance for human upliftment

➢ Rise beyond self for upliftment of citizens

11. Religious Wing

➢ Promote an attitude of accommodation for various religions

➢ Stress the parallel points to promote global peace

12. Scientists and Engineers Wing

➢ Stimulates the creation of new ideas for sustainable environment

➢ Integrate the role of spirituality in science and technology for self-fulfilling life

13. Security Services Wing

➢ Cope with anxiety during distress and strengthen innate virtues for effective making effective decisions during challenging situations

14. Shipping, Aviation and Tourism Wing

➢ Promote peace with the surge in international trade relations

15. Social Service Wing

➢ Strengthening the impoverished through spiritual realisation

➢ Collaborate with social workers for physical, moral and social betterment

16. SpARC Wing

➢ Research on the understanding of the physical and metaphysical world

➢ Researchers conduct experiments and share ideas through electronic forums

17. Sports Wing

➢ Development of inner strength of mind for maximal concentration

18. Transport and Travel Wing

➢ Enhance self-control to avoid drugs, alcohol and anger

➢ Harness inner potentials to apply spiritual principles to their jobs

19. Women Wing

➢ Make women conscious of their potentials while incrementing men's awareness of females' contributions

➢ Combat social evils of obscene media and disparate treatment of women

➢ Elevate the power of the soul comprised in both the genders

20. Youth Wing

➢ Promote the involvement of youth in community service

➢ Inspire to live a life of discipline, sacrifice, simplicity and purity

Row to success

One notion that is clear from all the statements made about teamwork is that good teams don't just work together. One is not a charioteer who just gives directions and pulls reins deeming his members as horses, rather they are rowers. An ideal team rows the boat along with other rowers to move the boat down the course to reach the finish line. If you are an Indian, you must have witnessed the sight of 100 players on massive snake boats, either in movies or on your visit to Kerala, rowing in the annual competition of Vallam kali held during the harvest festival of Onam.

So, what is that which really intrigued me about the game of rowing and its relation to teamwork? Well, everybody is fascinated by the marching bands and parades that take place all over the world. The uniformity of their strides, the cadence of their percussion and the joint efforts are apparently the elements that entice us, providing a feeling of contentment. Likewise, rowing is a game of synchronised movements. When varied employees with dynamic skills orient their objectives together, those collaborative endeavours help attain success. Teamwork makes the plan work. A leader may emerge in the process but a leader is as much a worker as any other team member. He is the person who directs the sail and acts as a coxswain when needed. A coxswain in rowing coordinates the power and rhythm of rowers while steering the boat.

An individual has different skill sets, the ability to align the required skills towards an aim is what makes a team work for your own being. The rowers are your capabilities and senses. The ship of your life has to be sailed alone. You might meet other travellers who may provide you with a map, but remember that you hold the oars. The command over your distractions lies in your mind, choose to feed your discipline, not toxins that may engender a hole and make you drown.

When one domino of your life falls, every member of your inner team starts dropping. Most of the time it doesn't even matter to people when you are off from the world for two days, it is you who has to push and stop the dominos from falling. Take command of your team.

Choose your hard

When working in a team, a person's ideas may not always be on the same page with that of others. Initially, doing things accordingly may sound hard but the belief in the greater good will keep you moving. Sacrificing your comforts and contrasting viewpoints become inconvenient. Tackling the issues of your wrong moves comes at the price of alienation and disappointment. Coordination is a tug of war.

Hold onto the objectives of a team?
Let loose to crash the dream?
Choose your hard.

Understanding Shades of Humanity

Empathy

Life is a canvas of different hues; it's an art and the art of life is different for everyone. The paintings on a canvas may be as easy to comprehend as a scenery or as puzzling to decipher as abstract art. Whatever may be the art on your canvas, it's as unique as the stripes on a tiger. We humans share the common colour of orange-yellow of humanity, with our stripes establishing our individual identities on this planet. If you are unable to interpret the art of another person, try to hold his hand, follow the strokes of his brush and see where the colours got mixed, understand the world from his eyes, that's empathy.

I believe that a soul is gifted with colours before it enters the womb. Our tiny hands hold them. Gradually as we grow, our palms fold, the colours get opened up, and they mingle to form different shades. Creases on our palms make the lines of our fate which are coloured with these paints. That's how you become one in a billion.

Life is like a balanced blend of bright flowers in the tulip garden of Amsterdam against the pastel sky. It is dark and sooty for a person born in the cage of poverty. A book, the sparkling sun and the glistening water of the turquoise sea, life seems perfect with pastels. Blues and whites of the hospital sights, the black reaper lurks around the corner. If you cannot alleviate someone's condition, the least yet the greatest help would be to offer a shade of listening, a colour of reassurance and even an extra brush of strength.

We at Brahma Kumaris greet each other with *Om Shanti*. It is the first basis of establishing empathy which means "I" this soul is at peace, lighter beyond the consciousness of the body. When an individual is soul conscious, he transcends the bondages and limitations of the mind to perceive the situation with love and kindness. Empathy requires you to not offer an umbrella to a person in rain but stand together with him to feel the rain.

Jelly - A sweet solution for connection

In the city of Ciara, there lived three friends, Jelly, Marble and Rocky. Once, Mrs. Lee lost her pet cat which she adored dearly. In her lonely life, her cat was her stick of old age. Rocky found her utterly devastated while on his way home. Upon knowing the matter, he said, "What's the big deal Mrs. Lee? Find another cat, as simple as that."

Mrs. Lee put up lost posters around the town across various locations. Marble at the sight of this, instantly helped her to stick the posters around. While consoling her, he replied with - "I am sorry about your lost cat. Don't worry, even if we don't find it, you will be fine in a few days."

Jelly noticed the downhearted Mrs. Lee sitting idly on a bench in the park. She knew about her missing cat from her friends. In order to make her feel good, Jelly brought her coffee and lilacs. After offering her these things, she sat beside her and narrated the story of how she lost her soft toy which was a bunny, gifted to her by her grandfather on her 3rd birthday. Jelly said, "I know it has been tough for you since the past few days, Mrs. Lee. I understand the value of losing something valuable. You have done all you could. I am here to help you find it and provide you with company whenever you need me."

You will meet different kinds of people in life and you will have a choice to become the person you want to be. Rocky displayed the absence of concern for a person who was dejected. His indifferent attitude lacked compassion. On the other hand, while Marble expressed the feelings of pity and stood up for help, he was sympathetic. Jelly was the person who felt the heart of Mrs. Lee about her unfortunate situation. She understood her feelings, tried to relate with her experience and provided her with assurance.

Rocky was cold, stiff and did not care about others feelings. Marble acknowledged the situation and tried to provide a fix which seemed unreasonable. Jelly validated the feelings of Mrs. Lee and resonated with her emotions. Don't be rigid like Rocky or get the situation but leave the bits of acceptance like Marble. Mould yourself like Jelly to build a connection.

The Unmatched shade of empathy - Mother

A mother never falls short of forming the tapestry of love and empathetic understanding. The genes of unconditional love and care never age. The hands of a mother get wrinkled as they grow old, but the cells of kindness never shrink. Mothers have the unfathomable amount of courage which equips them with the strength to perform selfless actions. This courage is the driving force behind them being able to empathise with their children.

The motherly figure of Dadi Janki Ji, when asked by Sister Hansa whether it was important for her to attend the programme, given her 100 years of age and physical health, this is what she replied with,

"If I maintain courage, I know that God will help me.
(रहमते बच्चे मददे बाप)"

After witnessing the aftermath my surgery had on my mental health along with the reappearance of some past memories, my mom understood the situation and realised that I needed professional help to cope up with my panic attacks. She acknowledged the fact that even after providing me with the warmth of her presence, she was helpless in improving it. Dad stepped up too. They did not engage in questioning me and took me to the psychiatrist without making it weird. This was the brightest shade of empathy in my life when I was not treated as a victim but a teenager who just needed to hold her hand.

A tiny tale
She, a renowned artist and a very strict mother often scolded her 6-year-old for he could never draw a straight line. As he breathed slowly on the ventilator, she begged him every second to make a crook line on the ECG.

A mother will change her ideologies when she sees her child in suffering. Mould yourself like a mom who gets up early to prepare tiffin for you, one who skips her day at work because you were ill, one who tilts her umbrella towards you so that you don't get drenched, one who learns to make the perfect protein shake so that you don't get late and the one who will always wait for you when the world will leave you. Why? Because empathy to mothers is like white colour to an artist.

Hues of Honesty

Honesty is not about committing your mistakes with pride, rather it is the truthful and sincere acceptance of the faults you made and the shortcomings you failed to overpower. A shade of honesty is developed only when it is mixed with the colour of humility. Your greatness does not lie in the extravagant portrayal of being honest but being humble to stay true to your roots. Remember, dishonesty is not the concealment of reality from others but a theft of your virtues. You do not deceive others, but yourself.

The pangs of a heart made of deceit makes you bleed internally with guilt.

Honesty is a significant shade in the palette of empathy. One cannot attain the power to perceive another's situation genuinely from their eyes until their own eyes are fogged with amoral clouds.

Dadi Janki Ji used to say that God is pleased with an honest heart. With your power of realisation, place your honest heart in front of the Father. By doing so, your heart will become devoid of all the trash that has been rotting inside of you. A clear heart will then enable clear thoughts to flourish. An honest heart does work with good intentions without the slightest feeling of gaining anything in return. This altruistic trait is achieved when you rise above the physical traits of your body to be soul-conscious. The Supreme Father is the bestower. When you approach him with a pure heart, he is ever-ready to help you.

Karma never loses its address.

The hues of honesty got well amalgamated when during the initial years in London, the newly joined members could not wake early for *Amrit vela* or got late for the *Murli* class but still confessed their flaws. Dadi Janki used to sit those souls down with her personally and lovingly explained to them that even though they missed the golden hour of morning meditation, they can ensure to take out an hour from the day to recover it. She did not criticise or scold them, rather her motherly behaviour formed a connection that made things easy.

Spectrum of Thoughts

Thoughts are the building blocks of your mind. They are stacked one above the other and one negative thought has the capacity to demolish the tower of optimism that you build up. Keep the lines of intellect on your forehead straight. Do not allow it to get strained with the dark colours of bluff, gloom and treachery. Talk about good things today and leave the bad things for tomorrow.

Construct the castle of your life with positive thoughts, build it with bricks of belief and cement it with strength.

Only when you are in the possession of powerful vibrations, can you identify with others viewpoints. An empathetic heart will only culture when you are not drowned in the stream of hopelessness. Empathy instils motivation and hope in the distressed. When individuals see that you are able to navigate their paths by walking in their shoes, cooperation will follow these footsteps.

The immense power that thoughts hold can be seen through the various initiatives taken by Brahma Kumaris. Yogic Farming incorporates the might of thoughts to result in improved food quality and the enhanced emotional well-being of farmers. Patients with coronary blockages have reported clearance in their blood vessels after the constant practice of Rajyoga Meditation and positive affirmations.

The workers at corporate companies often witness a friction between their varied ideas and thoughts. Negative built up of energy will only elevate the situation and create further tension. Go in a state of silence before you reply to the provoking made by others, do not react. There is a broad line of difference between reaction and reply which people often tend to blur out. Reaction is the instant response to an event while reply is the thoughtful answer to a situation. Next time you find yourself in the middle of a conflict or depreciation, have empathy for other people's behaviour. It may be a consequence of their tensed life or pent-up emotions. Emerge the virtue of your thoughtfulness with the power of silence.

Love's Palette

The virtues of benevolence, courage, hope, purity and strength unify together to make up the palette of Love which is the indispensable part of Empathy. When Dadi Janki Ji went to London, her lectures were not understood by the foreigners due to language barriers. But her aura and speech held such powerful vibrations that the souls would get kindled and enlightened. Even if they did not understand the words, they would feel her love and catch her vibrations. Love has the power to rise above the limitations of the mind and the body. It is felt from the heart and not analysed through the brain.

Do you know about mitosis? It is the biological process through which cells divide. It is also done to replace worn out cells from the body. Love has a mitotic effect. It proliferates as you radiate warmth. It has the capacity to replace the worn-out parts of others, heal them.

Love and kindness are contagious.

As beautiful is the colour of love, it is difficult to make it because pretty things don't come easy. Anger and hate rise like the bubbles in wine, fast. Love needs time and it gradually picks up all its shades in the process. There can be harmony when one sets himself free from the bondages of unnecessary thoughts. Be the reason someone smiles today and not curse you for months.

In our daily *Murli* (spiritual reading), God teaches us that we should not dwell on other's weaknesses. By contemplating on the shortcomings of another individual, we accumulate their garbage in our intellect which spoils our minds. Mamma, also known as Saraswati (Goddess of Knowledge) always emphasised on paying heed to one's own efforts rather than the *Sanskars* (manners) of others. Hatred grows like an algal bloom when one clings onto the flaws of others. Disgust and anger are the aftermath of this poison.

Anger is in the bright shade of red that ignites the negative schema inside of you. It is the Venus Flytrap that traps your mind, digesting your goodwill making you lethal for yourself. Just like this plant, it provokes a reaction from you within seconds with its sensitive trigger hair. You lose the ability to pause and reply.

Making your way out of this trap is difficult but not impossible. An eminent sage once said, "How can there be peace on earth if the hearts of men are like volcanoes?" Anger jails you behind the bars of lost self-control. One has to revive and realise the inner strength of the mind to control the actions and thoughts. You are the owner of yourself. Don't let situations make you their slave.

The same water that reacts with calcium to form a white precipitate, flames with sodium. It is what you are made of, not the circumstances that define you.

It begins with the realisation that you have the capability to control it. You cannot take charge of other people's behaviours and situations but you are definitely the master of your own senses and actions. You must have come across these statements on a regular basis: "I don't like the way she talks and gets on my nerves every time", "How many times will I have to teach you this?", "We have to work extra time because he is always late." One important lesson I have learnt in the vicious cycle of rage is that the words I choose become the house I live in. Use of pessimistic vocabulary augments the situation and radiates anti-vibrations.

Choose to keep the gates of internal chaos closed and don't act on impulse. You never know the number of times a person feels your words when you act out in fury. Don't become a slave of anger. We allow anger to outweigh our virtue of love. Be a soul-conscious being who realises to focus on the more productive parts without getting imprisoned in quick judgements.

Be the catalyst of love, not the cancer of hate.

Love was the source of inspiration for the British singer and songwriter, Robin Gibb, a member of the popular musical group BeeGees who wrote a song "Mother of Love" for Dadi Janki. It was her scintillating aura and unconditional love that made people find hope. Love with a pure heart. Correct your belief or change your opinion when you encounter being biased due social conditions and public approval. Don't let the trait of being polite flicker. You should not change your colours for varied individuals, respectful with one and egoistic with another. Rather camouflage yourself with others to view the world from their glasses of life.

Empathy follows the steps of love. When you encounter a person anxious, irritated, low or less productive, have a chat with him, lend him your ears, give him time to cross the bridge of trust and open up. Provide the love one needs and the regard for his emotions. May love feel like a hot cup of cocoa on winter days, warm and to be with you.

Painted in Forgiveness

Forgiveness is freedom. It is an art *for giving* peace to your mind. To forgive is to break the chains of being hostage to your past. We are beautiful with our flaws, which means that we will make errors in our journey of life. Forgive yourself for the days when you put on a mask to confront reality and when you unintentionally hurt the people around you while the demons gnawed you from the inside.

God knows everything. Confessing our mistakes in front of him, even after knowing the fact that he knows it all is honesty. The One is the kindest of all, he embraces your imperfections when you have the integrity to accept your faults. He listens and forgives you as his dear child with an open heart.

A knife stabs you every time you make a mistake. Forgiveness is the power to pull out that knife and the fortitude to not stab it to someone else. You truly forgive yourself when you choose to analyse what went wrong and not infect others with your suffering. Do not let your vices overpower you.

Life is like an ice-cream. Repent and revert to your true self before your life melts.

It seems like a tough process during the initial stages of forgiveness. Loads of questions hover your mind but you have got the virtue to forgive and let go of things. Have you ever organised your stationery drawer to find that one ink pen or did you clean your wardrobe in the search for that one shirt? Just like these similar cases, your ethics lie behind the mess of futile thoughts.

Don't let the perceptions of the past actions put a label on people. Take one step forward towards your inherent goodness and God shall build you the rest of the bridge towards joy and contentment.

Take the three surfaces of water, slate and stone. A line drawn on water disappears immediately whereas a line drawn on a slate takes effort to remove it from a duster. The line etched on a stone is the hardest to remove. Select your surface wisely. Do you want to release these things easily, like water, or remain engraved with the past to affect your future? Having resentment punctures a hole in the gut, the hydrochloric acid then burns you instead of the bacteria. You bleed, which incapacitates your ability to have empathy for yourself. It deprives you to accept the conditions others go through, to feel the storm they went through. Be a band-aid of silver lining to the dark clouds, thus healing fast.

So, should we always tolerate the mistakes of others? Letting go of the faults of others should not come at the price of your righteousness. The price of French Fries elevates from100 bucks in an eatery to 500 bucks in an airport. The amount may rise to above an astonishing thousand in a 5-star restaurant. In similar fashion, you are valued differently by various people in your life. Forgiveness is not always about accepting or excusing the other person's behaviour. It is about letting go to prevent their actions from wounding your heart. Distance yourself from these places but don't overlook your errors.

Forgiving is a virtue. Forgetting is a strength. It is a decision to reclaim your life.

Some Shades of Empathy

Practising empathy may not always involve understanding a person only in adverse situations. There's more to it which includes assuring a person that you care and that their presence matters.

- We will find the light together.
- Your scars are the glitter that make your body sparkle.
- I made a playlist for you.
- I will protect this piece of your heart.
- Will you tell me about gardening Grandma? What did you water besides love?
- My shoulder will be your pillow, my ears your diary, come to me, don't be alone.
- Your presentation today at work was great!

- Your smile is the Dior of your attire, expensive and impressive.
- Dad, I am coming home. Looking forward to our long drive with retro songs and having green tea.
- Today's coffee smelled like your company. How have you been?
- I remember you like your fries with salsa sauce.
- You did not put a gratitude note today on your way back home, is everything ok?
- Let's go for a walk Grandpa.

Choose your hard

Being empathetic involves mirroring the feelings that one felt and the circumstances one encountered. It is the potential to deeply connect with others. Empathy entails taking the shape of the container you are put into. It poses a challenge to truly understand a person who has differing values than you. Albeit, each one has a different canvas of life, the primary colours remain perpetual. On the contrary, lack of an empathetic attitude cuts through your skin and leaves you alienated in the long-run.

Be like sand?
Be like gravel?
Choose your hard.

Small is Big

Organisational Skills

Have you ever been mesmerised by a butterfly's beauty? As it flutters gracefully in a garden, it captures the ephemeral beauty of nature in flight. Initially, the tiny egg is not aware of its capability to become a masterpiece of nature's artistry, unfolding its fragile wings. Similar is the case with us humans. Each one of us possesses skills that are waiting to be discovered and polished. It is about the small beginnings, a dollop of courage, a scoop of desire and extravagant portions of discipline.

While a butterfly typically takes about 4 weeks to develop into a functional adult, our learning process may take months or even years. The question is, are you consistent? Your growth should not be a stagnant lake, but rather an ever-ascending graph. The life-cycle of a butterfly demonstrates how it progresses from an egg to a caterpillar who constantly strives hard against the challenges of nature. Following this, the chrysalis (pupa) gets ready to finally develop into an adult, its beauty a testament to the magic of transformation. Likewise, your progress may be slow but it should be constant.

Organisation skills are the final gear that propels you towards achieving your aim. It entails managing your time and resources effectively on a daily basis to strive for the top. Small practices shape you into a resilient character who faces storms, tightens the ropes on the mast, and keeps sailing for larger endeavours.

Until you dive into the water, you will never truly grasp its depth or discover the extent of your own abilities. Available resources won't be beneficial until you don't ask for help and try to build yourself around it, much like, you can never learn driving if the car rests in your garage.

Sun has no effect on fake flowers,
Dreams without actions break towers.

Tiny steps, Great leaps

Do you think only your high-school education is important for your career ahead? Well, it was the alphabets and numbers at kindergarten that formed the base for us being categorised as *Homo sapiens*, species with complex brains to interact with their surroundings. This is the smallest step you take in the learning process to prepare you to enter into the larger world.

We have a habit of leaving things half undone, be it studying for Maths in school, learning a new language or graduating from college. We justify our actions and less productivity with, "If this much is sufficient, then why should I do more?" Getting just average marks in the subjects you don't like, trying on swimming only to discover you are no good will make you part of the crowd. Success walks to those who are ready to run the extra mile. While some of us learn fast, others have a slower pace. However, that doesn't mean you cannot do it, you just need some extra fertilisers and more exposure to sunlight to bloom. How do we know if the thing we are putting work into is worth our time? When trying doesn't tire you, when failures disappoint you but never become locks and when little improvements fuel you with unwavering determination, that's the moment you realise that your micro changes will result in macro success. When you know, you know.

Do not confuse this with the inherent talents. Some of the art is polished and not acquired just like, acting is refined with training and moves are mastered with more sessions of practice in dancing. But other skills with perfect practice can make you perfect. Consistency is like driving down a road with the same eucalyptus trees, leading you steadily to the enchanting destination at the end. The task is to not get bored and keep moving.

Remain a student until you can become a teacher
Give exams until you can become the examiner

Even if your interests alter with life, make sure the time you invested in a thing gives you a profitable return. My mom always says to put 100% effort into everything you do, no matter how small it seems as the learning will be immense.

Prosthetic Leg - A story of ambition

A crash, a life and a leg, that's what Aven lost one dark night. The death of his wife and his four-year-old daughter's amputated leg fragmented his castle of love. Facing the agony of loss and the haunting sound of machines beeping as Elena lay motionless on the hospital bed, shattered more strength inside of him than any truck could. The only hope that revived him was Elena's radiant smile when she said, "Small seeds, Dad."

Aven began juggling between multiple roles: Executive Director at work, a caring father on school runs, a comforting mother during night terrors, and a homemaker striving to keep the house a home. Little Elena, struggling with her prosthetic leg, found that the moves she had once mastered became steps she now wobbled on. She had always been passionate about dancing, and watching her grow up, Aven's heart broke into pieces every time she cried from not being able to perform better. But they did not stop, step by step they kept moving because they knew they could make it. Aven got help from his mother, learned how to manage things at home, organised his tasks at office and ensured to be with Elena for an hour when she practised. With physiotherapy and devoted amounts of practice, Elena started managing her life with her metallic limb.

But life has never been a smooth road, she started experiencing phantom limb pain, a perception of pain in a limb that no longer exists. Her old prosthetic leg made her feel disgusted. As the crucial contest loomed, the void left by her mother felt deeper than ever before. Aven found it unbearable to witness his daughter's anguish, a hurt he couldn't find the words to comfort. But every cloud has a silver lining. He discovered a high-tech artificial leg and had it engraved with two words said by his wife. Elena danced more flawlessly than ever with her new limb, captivating the audience and clinching the contest victory. In her heartfelt acceptance speech, she said, "Small seeds, Dad. Mom would be so proud to see the mighty trees we have become."

Just like small seeds, we face hardships but it is the endurance to keep progressing little by little that we blossom into something beautiful. The mechanical leg was Elena's ambition to do the extra to be extraordinary. What's your prosthetic leg?

Each one, Each day, Each rupee

Brahma Kumaris exemplify the incredible power of small efforts in creating big impacts.

Gyan Sarovar

Nestled amongst the Aravali Hills in Rajasthan, Gyan Sarovar (Lake of Knowledge) is a global village complex with a touch of modernity. With the surge in the number of followers and spread of service abroad, Brahma Kumaris established this campus to welcome souls from all walks of life. In 1993, Dr. Chenna Reddy, the governor of Rajasthan, while laying the foundation stone of its construction announced the donation of 5 lakh rupees. Dadi Prakashmani Ji, the then Administrative Head of the BKs, politely refused him with the introduction of the "Each one, Each day, Each rupee" movement. There were 3 lakh members during that time, out of which 60% of them were estimated to donate a rupee regularly for 2 months. With the grace of the Supreme Father, after three months, 10% amount required to avail for a loan was accumulated. This spiritual paradise was inaugurated in 1996.

Renowned as an "Academy for a Better World", it is an epitome of sustainability and technological innovation. With only 12% of the land covered with buildings, it has large lush green gardens blooming with fruits and flowers. The campus incorporates solar energy, wastewater treatment plant and aids recycling practices. Generating employment for the ruralites, Gyan Sarovar is the Headquarter for managing international services and is a residence for foreign followers during their stay.

Shantivan

Employing the same method, this complex has several buildings to accommodate 20,000 people while providing them with all the needed amenities. The chief attraction, Diamond Hall, measures 1 Lakh Square Feet and has the capacity to seat 20,000 individuals with no pillars to obstruct the view. This spiritual oasis features various meditation spaces, lecture halls, a museum, printing press and varied departmental buildings.

Starting the collection with a meagre amount of a rupee each day, projects worth crores were achieved successfully and continue to remain being operated in an efficacious manner. These examples are evidence that small efforts may not provide you with immediate success but get pooled to result in the attainment of a larger aim.

Kalp Taruh

It is a plantation project that combines human values with the environment to sustain life-giving trees with its motive "1 Person - 1 Plant - 1 Planet". This initiative focuses on nurturing the tree as well as the soul through values. It is the collective responsibility of every dweller on earth to work towards protecting the planet. Brahma Kumaris under Kalp Taruh brought together people from various nations, age groups and religions to do their part in the well-being of nature and their true self.

JAM

Just-A-Minute meditation initiative by the Brahma Kumaris was a small initiative to enable people to devote a minute of their 24 hours in silence and positive thoughts, as well as an event to contribute to the United Nations International Peace Day. The batteries of our mind being discharged with unnecessary thoughts throughout the day. In order to reclaim the inner peaceful state of mind, we remain in silence to become aware of our thoughts and divert them into useful vibrations to charge and strengthen our mental muscles.

Little Bit More

What stops you from doing more? Less time? Problems in life? When you lose the remote of your life. Our electronic devices have one remote but we have replicated our remotes. New challenges emerge, sometimes bringing with them adversaries and the weight of past regrets and future anxieties, and here we stand, ready to hand over a remote control to each of them from our stock. We often fail to realise the enormous potential that the tiny light in the middle of our forehead holds, the power of the soul. Your excuses and lack of commitment is your mind overpowering your decision to do more. Don't allow situations and other people to regulate you as they want. You have read the book of your life; you are the main character that holds the power to shape a new conclusion.

Like weeds are an inevitable part of the garden, so are the problems in our life. One person might be struck with twenty arrows and still stand tall with a stoic expression, while another person might crumble in tears from the impact of just one. That doesn't mean one person's pain is any less than another's, and you can't use this as a reason to avoid coping with your situation. Much like how small changes can have a big impact, tiny problems accumulated may feel like a heavy backpack. Choose to lift off the weight instead of getting tangled in the web of issues. In the end, it is you who has to cut the web and look out for solutions. The seeds of tolerance shall grow only when you allow them to germinate and blossom into strength. Choose wisely.

I recently read somewhere, "If given a chance to go back and erase your bad memories, would you, do it? No, because it will erase who you are." Your challenging life has made you who you are today. The scars, the tears, they are the symbols of victory, when life forced you to give up but you didn't. The biggest healer is you yourself, so why not climb the mountain and reach the top? Take those steps which sound risky, fall but try because you will never know until you have begun and crossed the starting line.

The snow you slip on the first day will become the surface you glide on one day.

Another reason we fear to settle for the average is because we are affected by the results of others. Don't cage yourself behind the rods of someone else's success. Project your bar to break and overtake. Don't give people the authority to imprison you behind their standard of bars. Pretexts are the demons chaining you to failure. Push the doors closed with the excuses of your inabilities.

Do not measure your success with someone else's scale.

Value your worth, don't be an approval addict. Your value will not be established when others approve of your actions, it will be established when you believe in your work. Even if you charge 50 bucks initially, know that your skills deserve it. Don't lose yourself in pleasing people or for the sake of relationships. The true ones will always value you and stay by your side.

Have faith in your honest work and God will never leave your side. When you begin with your tiny beginnings, he will ensure that they have great outcomes. When intentions are pure, desires are fulfilled and every daunting obstacle is overcome.

Dieting for your distractions

Restraining from engaging in entertainment and leisure throughout the day will always feel like a burden. Devoting a set time to indulge in them will lead you to crave more and you will end up exceeding your limit just like when a person refraining himself from eating sugar to maintain his diet ends up consuming more of it when finally given the window.

Segregate your time slots into shorter spans to engage in leisurely activities. This will ensure that you get a necessary boost at a regular time without feeling monotonous in your work. The discipline to stick to your time slots is the remote of your mind, do you want to close it or indulge some more? Social media apps become toys on the cradle when you lose hold of your responsibilities. Sculpt your own life rather than being chiselled by others.

Choose your hard

As easy as it may sound, taking the small steps, inculcating the small habits is tough for days. Anything that displeases our brain, urges our mind to remain tucked in the quilt has the ability to make the *average* lurk around the corner. The journey of minor efforts is a long and monotonous path of consistency, but a giant leap to changes will flip your life to accommodate the discomforts.

Climb the stairs?
Jump the mountain?
Choose your hard.

75

76

Acknowledgements

Thank you, Baba, for always being there through my highs and lows. Your presence has given me the strength to stand where I am today.

"Let inner harmony compose the authentic notes of your life's melody." This is what my mentor said when he first inspired me with the idea of writing a book. Being a teenager then, he imparted to me the stark realities of navigating adult life. He emphasised that I have to step up my game before it is too late to just end up blending with the crowd. He said that an authentic self and a pure heart is a person's greatest strength. I am deeply grateful to Puneet Bhatia Sir for being the kind person he is and guiding me throughout the process. You placed your trust and belief in me so that I could kick start this journey, thank you.

To Dr. Shibani Basu Dubey, my teacher, who graciously set aside time from her busy schedule to aid me in editing my book, I extend my sincere thanks. Thank you to my grandparents who have always appreciated my creative process as a writer. To my friends who make my life better by being in it, thank you for always cheering me up.

My parents, who have never questioned my abilities and have always been a constant support in my endeavours. Dad, though you have stayed away from me due to work, never have you ever distanced yourself from being a father to me when I needed you the most. Mumma, I can never find the words to convey what an amazing woman you have been in my life; I draw my strength from you. Mom you are my heart and Dad my blood. From handling my odd vocabulary in childhood, to finally reading this book, thank you for being the loving parents you are.

 I love you.

To the readers, whom I have not met, I hope my words reached your core. Thank you for reading my work. I wish you a happy life that shines with your presence.

About the Author

Shubhi Sen is an aspiring author who loves her lattes as much as she loves letters. Her first 75-word letter to God when she was just four, planted the seeds for her writing journey. Being a part of Brahma Kumaris for 15 years, her mother first took her to their centre when she was just five months old. Her relationship with spirituality has deepened ever since she was embraced by the loving divine family.

When she was 6 years old, her uncle made her watch Ratatouille. Since then, the dialogue from the Disney movie, "Your only limit is your soul", has been etched in her mind to not let others define her capabilities.

Despite having a rugged life as a teenager, she believes that the people one encounters are the characters in the story of one's life. Some characters are permanent, while others are just good chapters – good chapters that need not have happy endings. What makes these chapters good is the experience they provide and a shield of strength they build.

She rediscovered the light of God, which imbued her with faith and the power to sculpt our lives with our own hands. Sen finds joy in the small, diverse pleasures of life, both in her daily routine and through her travels. It was literature that made her feel things more deeply, sparking her imagination and voicing through words.

Shubhi upholds the belief that some gates of opportunity are not locked; they are just stiff. One must exert extra effort to push them open.